Copyright © 2021 Erica Yueh

All rights reserved. No part of this book may be reproduced or used
in any manner without the prior written permission of the copyright owner.

Written By: Erica Yueh
Illustrations By: Mahnoor Ali
Published By: BookBaby

ISBN: --978-1-09838-197-4

For Kyler, my Universe.

I AM BEAUTIFUL
NO MATTER WHAT ANYONE SAYS,
I AM BEAUTIFUL.
DO YOU SEE ME?

I AM MEEK.
I AM LOYAL.
I AM TRUSTWORTHY.
DO YOU SEE ME?

I AM **RESPONSIBLE**.
I AM **HONEST**.
DO YOU SEE ME?

I AM THE FUTURE.
I CAN DO ANYTHING
I PUT MY MIND TO.
I CAN BE ANYTHING
I WANT TO BE. DO YOU SEE ME?

NO ONE CAN DEFINE ME.
I CAN ONLY BE ME.
I LOVE ME. DO YOU SEE ME?

My Daily Affirmations

_____

_____

_____

_____

_____

My Daily Affirmations

_____

_____

_____

_____

My Daily Affirmations

_____

_____

_____

_____

My Daily Affirmations

_____

_____

_____

_____

My Daily Affirmations

_____

_____

_____

_____

My Daily Affirmations

_____

_____

_____

_____

_____

My Daily Affirmations

_____

_____

_____

_____

My Daily Affirmations

_____

_____

_____

_____

My Daily Affirmations

_____

_____

_____

_____

_____

My Daily Affirmations

_____

_____

_____

_____

_____

My Daily Affirmations

_____

_____

_____

_____

My Daily Affirmations

_____

_____

_____

_____